PIANO • VOCAL

ORIGINAL KEYS FOR SINGERS

ISBN 0-7935-7573-7

7777 W. BLUEMOUND RD. P.O. BOX 13819 MILWAUKEE, WI 53213

Visit Hal Leonard Online at
www.halleonard.com

PATSY CLINE

Contents

PATSY CLINE

by Elaine Schmidt

When four-year-old Virginia Patterson Hensley won a talent contest by singing "On the Good Ship Lollipop," no one but her mother took her aspirations to stardom seriously. For the next twenty-six years, "Ginny" Hensley would chase her dream, despite daunting hardships and frequent setbacks. In the end, Ginny became one of America's first female country music stars, blazing a trail for an entire generation of female country musicians. She broke new ground as a crossover artist by simultaneously charting hits on *Billboard* magazine's country and pop charts. Virginia Hensley would come to be known as a brash, outspoken woman of legendary temper and generosity. She would create a vocal sound and style unlike anything else found in country music during the late 1950s and early 1960s, making recordings that would continue to sell more than thirty years after her death. Her turbulent life story would eventually be told in film, books, and a stage production. The world would come to know Virginia Hensley by the name Patsy Cline.

Ginny Hensley was born on September 8, 1932, in Gore, Virginia. Her parents had been married just six days before, in a "shotgun" wedding that Ginny's father Sam would always resent. Ginny's mother, Hilda Patterson, was sixteen at the time of the wedding and totally unprepared for life with her hard-drinking, abusive husband. Hilda and Patsy defended each other against Sam until he finally abandoned the family during Ginny's sophomore year in high school. Patsy had to leave school and take a job slaughtering chickens to help support the fatherless family, which by then included her siblings, Sam Jr. and Sylvia Mae. Ginny lost her slaughterhouse job when it was discovered that she was underage, eventually landing a job at the soda fountain of a local drugstore. She would often announce to friends and customers that she was going places, that she was going to be a star.

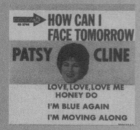

Ginny was determined to sing. At age fourteen she approached "Joltin' " Jim McCoy, a broadcaster on radio station WINC in Winchester, Virginia, announcing that she wanted to sing on his show. He was so struck by her boldness and determination that he gave her an audition. Although inexperienced, Ginny could sing and won over the WINC personnel. That same fearless determination would allow her to march up to various radio and television personalities over the years and ask to sing with their bands or appear in productions. She always asked for a chance to perform, never for an audition. Ginny's eyes were always on the future, and even at fourteen, she was dreaming of singing at the Grand Ole Opry.

For the time being, Ginny would keep her job at the drugstore, working all day Saturday and singing in the evening. Hilda would drive her to various towns, wherever Patsy could land a performance. Protective of her daughter, Hilda would usually stay at the club until 1:00 a.m., when Patsy's night was finished. Ginny eventually wrangled an introduction to Bill Peer, who sold cars by day and fronted the band Bill Peer and His Melody Boys and Girls by night. Peer and Ginny met at the Brunswick Moose Hall in 1952, forming a working relationship almost immediately. Peer added some glitz to Ginny's cowgirl costumes and created a new name for her using a shortened version of her middle name. Ginny began to perform under the name Patsy Hensley. Despite their age difference (she was twenty-one years old; he was thirty-two) and Peer's wife and children, Patsy and Peer immediately launched into a love affair. This was hardly young Patsy's first, nor would it be her last. Shortly after meeting Peer she also began an affair with Gerald Cline, who would soon become her first husband.

Married on March 7, 1953, Gerald and Patsy had problems from day one. Gerald wanted Patsy to stay at home and act the part of a dutiful wife. Patsy wanted to sing and was not about to allow a marriage to stand in her way. She continued her affair with Bill Peer until his wife divorced him and he began to pursue Patsy with ideas of marriage. The fall of 1955 saw the end of Patsy's personal and musical relationship with Peer, much to Peer's dismay. In April of 1955 Patsy, still married to Gerald, met Charlie Dick, quickly falling in love. On January 23, 1957, Gerald filed for divorce. That same year, on September 15, Patsy married Charlie Dick in an understated ceremony. Patsy and Charlie would have two children, Julia Simadore, who would be known as Julie, and Alan Randolph, who would be known as Randy. Although Charlie and Patsy claimed to love each other, the pair fought continually. The fighting began during their courtship and continued unabated throughout their marriage. Patsy frequently arrived for rehearsals sporting dark glasses and heavy makeup to cover bruises. In 1959 Patsy hooked up with guitarist/manager/amateur airplane pilot Randy Hughes. When Hughes and Patsy entered into a manager/client relationship, they began an affair as well.

Patsy took what she believed to be a step forward by signing a recording contract with 4 Star Records on September 30, 1954. It would instead prove to be both a musical and a financial fiasco. Bill McCall, owner of 4 Star Records, knew that the lion's share of money to be made in pop music was in the rights to songs. He made a practice of buying song rights from struggling songwriters who were only too glad for the cash fix offered by his $25 or $30 buy-out fees. McCall could work the system. In cases where he owned controlling rights to a song, he would often rework a few words in the lyrics so that he could give himself credit as co-writer and collect half of the song's copyright money. He often "wrote" these lyrics under the pen name

W.S. Stevenson, a combination of William Shakespeare's initials and Robert Louis Stevenson's surname. McCall then required the artists on his label to record only songs to which 4 Star held the rights. McCall's deal with Patsy provided her $50 up front for each song she recorded and 2.34 percent of the royalties. However, the stipulation in Patsy's contract that all studio and musician's fees were to be paid out of her royalties ensured that Patsy rarely saw a penny of royalty money. Her balance sheet with McCall was perpetually in the red, a fact compounded by Patsy's several requests for cash advances. McCall would grant the advance, but only if Patsy would sign an extension of her contract.

Patsy scored one big hit during her 4 Star days. When the song "Walkin' After Midnight" was presented to her in 1956, she hated it. Her response was characteristically blunt: "This song's got no balls." In the end Patsy was persuaded to record "Walkin' " by the promise that she could pick the song for the flip side of the recording. Recorded on November 8, 1956, "Walkin' After Midnight" was Patsy's first hit. After she promoted it on the "Arthur Godfrey's Talent Scouts" TV show, it quickly went to #2 on the *Billboard* country charts and #12 on the pop charts.

"I Fall to Pieces," was a another song Patsy disliked when she first heard it. In 1960 her contract with 4 Star ended, and she was signed to the Decca label. At Decca, under the guidance of Owen Bradley, Patsy had to be persuaded to record "I Fall to Pieces." At the recording session, Patsy's first take of the song included an octave jump on the last phrase to allow her to "belt" the ending. Bradley objected and they tried another take, in which she followed his instructions to keep the ending understated. "I Fall to Pieces" soared to the top of the charts. Patsy had proved that she was more than a one-hit wonder.

Patsy's fifty-ninth recording—her eighth for Decca—was another hit, and yet another song she detested at the outset. The composer, also the voice on the demo recording that Patsy heard, was a short-haired, suit-wearing new kid on the Nashville scene named Willie Nelson. Patsy hated the demo, hated the song, and had to be talked into recording it. She went for the recording on August 21, 1961, and couldn't come up with a take she liked. Finally Owen Bradley suggested that they record the background music and have Patsy come in later to do the lead vocal. She came back in on August 24 and got "Crazy" out of the way in one take. Once again a song she hated became a huge hit for her. In just six months' time, Patsy had gone from constant financial worry to dealing with the status and income of a star.

Patsy was nothing if not infuriating. She always saw herself as a country singer. She was a self-proclaimed hillbilly and proud of it. Even when managers and promoters suggested that she could reach a much larger audience by losing the western costumes and leaning toward pop, Patsy fought tooth and nail to retain her country image. Her tendency to show up for performances with liquor on her breath endeared her to no one, and her frequent tardiness got her fired from Jimmy Dean's "Town and Country Jamboree." Patsy liked to refer to herself as "the Cline" and called everyone, regardless of gender, "Hoss." She could scream in anger one minute, and then laugh it off the next. She could also be exceptionally warm-hearted and generous. Patsy had no cattiness toward other female country singers. She welcomed them to the fold, advising them and helping them whenever and wherever she could.

Patsy was a mentor to the naive Loretta Lynn, teaching her how to carry herself on stage and how to dress, giving her some appropriate clothing. When a very young Brenda Lee was stiffed by a promoter and stranded in Texas with her mother and no money, Patsy drove them back to Nashville in her car. Patsy once gave Dottie West a scrapbook of photos and memories into which she had tucked a check for $75 and a note explaining that she knew that Dottie and her husband were having a hard time; she wanted them to use the money to pay their rent. On a two-week tour with Johnny Cash and various other artists, Patsy discovered twelve-year-old Barbara Mandrell rooming by herself without a chaperon. Patsy arranged for the two of them to share a room for the duration of the tour, in order to look after the young girl.

Over the course of her short life, Patsy cheated death on several occasions. The first was a bout with rheumatic fever when the singer was thirteen. "I developed a terrible throat infection," she explained in 1957, "and my heart even stopped beating. The doctor put me in an oxygen tent. You might say it was my return to the living after several days that launched me as a singer. The fever affected my throat, and when I recovered I had this booming voice like Kate Smith's."

In 1959 Patsy had the first of two serious automobile accidents. She was reluctant to divulge details, possibly because she was at fault. In June of 1961 Patsy returned home for her sister Sylvia's high school graduation. While she was riding in a car driven by her brother Sam, an oncoming car pulled into their lane in order to pass another vehicle. The car hit them head-on, sending Patsy flying through the windshield. Two passengers in the other car were killed. Sam survived his serious injuries, and the driver of the other car walked away with cuts and bruises. Patsy had several fractures, a dislocated hip, and a badly gashed face. In critical condition for several days, she was not expected to live. Although she later underwent several operations to repair the facial damage, she was permanently scarred by the accident. The scars went deeper than she initially thought. While she

was recording "She's Got You" in December of 1961, she fell into fits of sobbing several times during the recording session. Later that month she was diagnosed as having suffered a nervous breakdown.

No matter how brash and self-assured Patsy may have seemed, there was a part of her that needed constant reassurances. After a recording session or concert, she would ask repeatedly if things had gone all right and if she had sounded okay. She could never hear enough praise. One of her great heartaches was that Winchester, the town in which she had spent a good part of her childhood, continually snubbed her. Too many people in town remembered her early days, when she shocked the community with flashy clothing and frequent affairs.

With success came a grueling schedule. On March 3, 1963, Patsy took time from her own concerts to perform in a benefit in Kansas City. A prominent D.J., known as "Cactus Jack" Wesley, had been killed in a car accident a few months earlier, and several country musicians put together the benefit for his widow and two small children. With son Randy sick at home, Patsy was anxious to get off the road, but agreed to add the Kansas City concert to the end of her tour. To save time, manager Randy Hughes flew Patsy, Hawkshaw Hawkins, and Lloyd "Cowboy" Copas to Kansas City in his small plane. Randy, Patsy, Cowboy, and Billy Walker intended to fly back the following morning, but bad weather changed their plans. Walker got word that his father had suffered a heart attack and wanted to return immediately. Hawkins offered him the ticket he held for a commercial flight, offering to wait out the weather and return with Hughes and company. Dottie and Bill West were packing their car to drive back to Nashville and offered Patsy a ride. Patsy initially agreed but then changed her mind, assuming that the weather would soon clear and she could get home faster with Randy.

Randy, who was not trained to fly by instrument readings, had to wait for clear weather in order to see well enough to fly safely. The group was unable to depart until 1:30 in the afternoon on March 5. They flew north into Arkansas and landed to wait for the weather in their path to clear. They took off again, landing in Dyersburg, Tennessee, about 140 miles from Nashville, at 5:20. Despite doubtful weather ahead, the plane took off for Nashville at 6:07. Randy flew his little plane straight into a severe storm. Placing an S.O.S. call at 6:22, Randy began to look for a place to land in the thickly wooded countryside below him. Randy was heard on the emergency radio saying, "Maybe I should fly low and follow a road." Then, "No, that's bad to do. It's better that I gain altitude." Blinded by fog, clouds, and rain, Randy lost his bearings completely. The last transmission recorded on the emergency radio was a voice crying out, "My God, Randy—we're flying upside down! Randy!"

When songwriter Roger Miller, a friend of Patsy's, heard that Randy's plane was missing, he drove to Camden, the area in which they were last heard from, arriving at about 6:00 a.m. Miller was the first person at the crash site. The plane had crashed nose first into the ground. Pieces of the plane and its passengers were scattered over a sixty-yard area. Bits of their costumes hung from the trees; shattered musical instruments littered the ground.

The press released word that the plane was missing, amending the story later with the news that four Opry stars had been killed. Details of the funeral arrangements were released as well. After Patsy's casket lay in state in her home for a day, as was her wish, it was sent to Winchester for a funeral that quickly became a circus. Fans and reporters converged for the ceremony. At the graveside, a fan pulled a flower from one of the many arrangements on hand. The action had a domino effect as fans rushed forward and pulled flowers from arrangements, eventually picking

them clean. Patsy Cline was buried at Shenandoah Memorial Park, beneath a headstone that read, "Virginia Dick 1932–1963."

Of the fifty-one songs Patsy recorded for Decca, only twenty-four had been released by the time of her death. Subsequent releases of "Sweet Dreams" b/w "Back in Baby's Arms" and "Faded Love" b/w "When You Need a Laugh" kept her name on the charts for several years. In 1980 and '81, re-releases of two of her singles made it onto the country charts. In 1985, Jessica Lange played Patsy in the successful film biography *Sweet Dreams.* More recently, a musical version of Patsy's story, entitled *Always...,* appeared at small theaters around the country, opening Off-Broadway in June of 1997.

Being a card-carrying member of the Grand Ole Opry was one of Patsy's earliest dreams. She made her debut on the famous radio show on July 1, 1955, becoming a member in January of 1960. Over the course of her short career, Patsy also played Carnegie Hall and the Hollywood Bowl, appeared on "Arthur Godfrey's Talent Scouts" (Godfrey canceled her scheduled appearance on "The Ed Sullivan Show," not wanting to share his "find"), "The Bob Crosby Show," "Town Hall Party," and a host of other nationally broadcast programs and scores of regional shows. Patsy won the star status she spoke about while working at the drugstore soda fountain, but at tremendous personal cost. She bought herself a dream house, which she adored, but her performing schedule left her little time to enjoy it. In retrospect, Patsy's 1962 quote to a high school newspaper in Peoria, Illinois, serves as a poignant epitaph. She said, "I've gotten more than I asked for. All I ever wanted was to hear my voice on record and have a song among the Top 20."

PatsyCline

BACK IN BABY'S ARMS

Words and Music by
BOB MONTGOMERY

Happily, with a bounce (in 2)

ALWAYS

Words and Music by
IRVING BERLIN

BLUE MOON OF KENTUCKY

Words and Music by
BILL MONROE

Medium straight-eighth Rock-a-billy

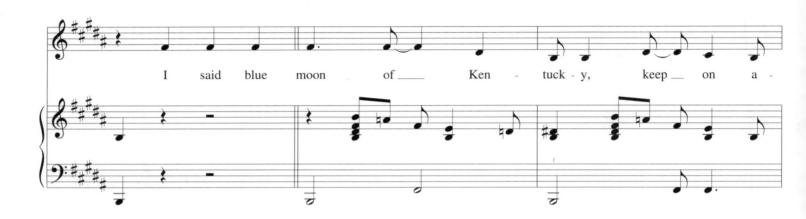

I said blue moon of ___ Ken - tuck - y, keep ___ on a -

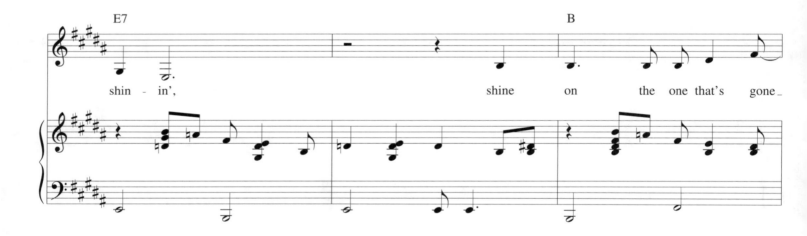

shin - in', shine on the one that's gone ___

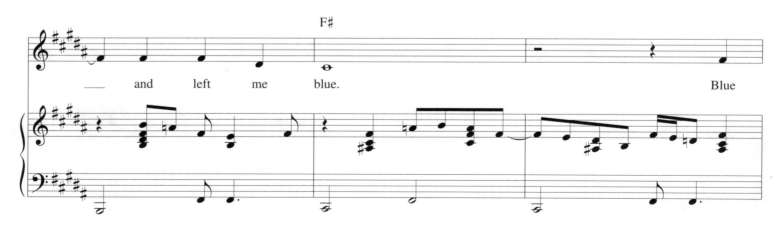

___ and left me blue. Blue

FOOLIN' 'ROUND

Words and Music by HARLAN HOWARD
and BUCK OWENS

D.S. al Coda

CODA

when it's you ___ a fool I'll al - ways

be. I know that

me. So ___

hon - ey, fool ___ a - round you know right where I'm at. ___

CRAZY

Words and Music by
WILLIE NELSON

FADED LOVE

Words and Music by BOB WILLS
and JOHNNY WILLS

HALF AS MUCH

Words and Music by
CURLEY WILLIAMS

HAVE YOU EVER BEEN LONELY?
(Have You Ever Been Blue?)

Words by GEORGE BROWN
Music by PETER DeROSE

HE CALLED ME BABY

Words and Music by
HARLAN HOWARD

Moderately

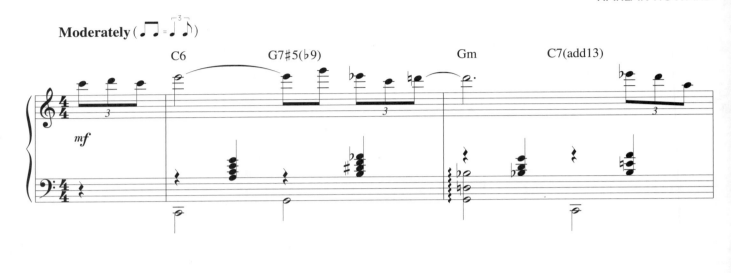

He called me ba — by,

ba - by all night long, _____ used to

I FALL TO PIECES

Words and Music by HANK COCHRAN
and HARLAN HOWARD

IT WASN'T GOD WHO MADE HONKY TONK ANGELS

Words and Music by
J.D. MILLER

I Love You So Much It Hurts

Words and Music by
FLOYD TILLMAN

JUST A CLOSER WALK WITH THEE

Traditional
Arranged by KENNETH MORRIS

LOOSE TALK

Words and Music by FREDDIE HART
and ANN LUCAS

68

A POOR MAN'S ROSES
(Or a Rich Man's Gold)

Words by BOB HILLIARD
Music by MILTON DeLUGG

SHE'S GOT YOU

Words and Music by
HANK COCHRAN

SO WRONG

Words and Music by CARL PERKINS,
MEL TILLIS and DANNY DILL

STRANGE

Words and Music by MEL TILLIS
and FRED BURCH

Rhumba-feel

Strange ____ how you stopped lov-ing me,
Strange ____ you _ changed like ____ night and day,

how you stopped need-ing me ____ when _ she came
just up and walked a - way ____ when _ she came

SWEET DREAMS

Words and Music by
DON GIBSON

Sweet _____ dreams of you _____ ev - 'ry night _____ I go through

Why can't _____ I for - get you and

THREE CIGARETTES IN AN ASHTRAY

Words and Music by EDDIE MILLER
and W.S. STEVENSON

TRUE LOVE

Words and Music by
COLE PORTER

WALKIN' AFTER MIDNIGHT

Words and Music by DON HECHT
and ALAN BLOCK

WHEN I GET THROUGH WITH YOU
(You'll Love Me Too)

Words and Music by
HARLAN HOWARD

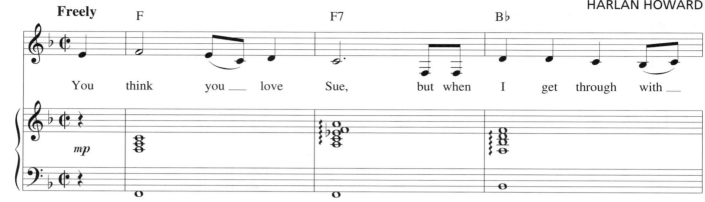

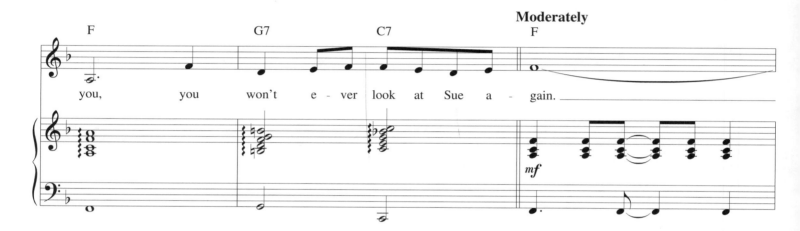

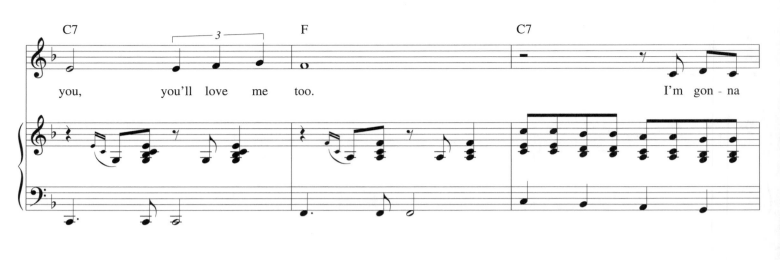

you, you'll love me too. I'm gon-na

treat you so sweet __ and kind, I'll drive her right

out of your mind, And you won't know her if __ you meet,

walk right by her on __ the street. Be-cause I want you and

WHY CAN'T HE BE YOU

Words and Music by
HANK COCHRAN

YOU BELONG TO ME

Words and Music by PEE WEE KING,
REDD STEWART and CHILTON PRICE

You're Stronger Than Me

Words and Music by HANK COCHRAN
and JIMMY KEY

YOUR CHEATIN' HEART

Words and Music by
HANK WILLIAMS